THE
ECONOMIC
FUTURE
OF CITY
AND
SUBURB

DAVID L. BIRCH

COMMITTEE FOR ECONOMIC DEVELOPMENT

Single copy $1.25

THE

ECONOMIC

FUTURE

OF CITY

AND

SUBURB

The Author

DAVID L. BIRCH is Assistant Professor of Business Administration at the Harvard Business School. After graduating from Harvard College in 1959, he joined RCA Corporation as Supervisor of Project Operations, and later served as Management Analyst for the NASA Goddard Space Flight Center. He received his M.B.A. from the Harvard Graduate School of Business Administration in 1962 and joined the staff of General Dynamics/Astronautics as a Research Engineer. Birch returned to the Harvard Business School in 1963 as a Research Assistant and became a Research Associate in 1964. At the same time, he also held the position of Research Engineer at the California Institute of Technology/Jet Propulsion Laboratory. After receiving his doctorate in 1966, Birch was appointed Assistant Professor. He is affiliated with the Kennedy Institute of Politics as a member of the Faculty Study Group on Poverty in Massachusetts. He has also served as an advisor to the Committee for Economic Development. Birch is the author of *The Businessman and the City*.

THE
ECONOMIC
FUTURE
OF CITY
AND
SUBURB

DAVID L. BIRCH

COMMITTEE FOR ECONOMIC DEVELOPMENT

CED Supplementary Paper Number 30

Printed in the U.S.A.
First Printing, 1970
Second Printing, 1972
Third Printing, 1973
COMMITTEE FOR ECONOMIC DEVELOPMENT
477 Madison Avenue, New York, N.Y. 10022
Library of Congress Catalog Card Number: 74-127247
International Standard Book Number: 0-87186-230-1

A CED SUPPLEMENTARY PAPER

This Supplementary Paper is issued by the Research and Policy Committee of the Committee for Economic Development in conformity with the CED Bylaws (Art. V, Sec. 6), which authorize the publication of a manuscript as a Supplementary Paper if:

a) It is recommended for publication by the Project Director of a subcommittee because in his opinion, it "constitutes an important contribution to the understanding of a problem on which research has been initiated by the Research and Policy Committee" and,

b) It is approved for publication by a majority of an Editorial Board on the ground that it presents "an analysis which is a significant contribution to the understanding of the problem in question."

This Supplementary Paper relates to the Statement on National Policy, *Reshaping Government in Metropolitan Areas,* issued by the CED Research and Policy Committee in February 1970.

The members of the Editorial Board authorizing publication of this Supplementary Paper are:

This paper has also been read by the Research Advisory Board, the members of which under the CED Bylaws may submit memoranda of comment, reservation, or dissent.

While publication of this Supplementary Paper is authorized by CED's Bylaws, except as noted above its contents have not been approved, disapproved, or acted upon by the Committee for Economic Development, the Board of Trustees, the Research and Policy Committee, the Research Advisory Board, the Research Staff, or any member of any board or committee, or any officer of the Committee for Economic Development.

CED RESEARCH ADVISORY BOARD

Foreword

A decade ago, CED published Raymond Vernon's *The Changing Economic Function of the Central City*. The Vernon paper dramatically illustrated the increasing economic disadvantage of the central city as well as the economic interdependence between city and suburb. The research contained in this supplementary paper, written by David L. Birch at the request of the Subcommittee on Metropolitan Government in the Federal System, builds upon that earlier study as is likewise true of the subcommittee's recommendations in the recent policy statement, *Reshaping Government in Metropolitan Areas*.

Taking his theme from the economic disadvantages of central cities outlined in the Vernon paper, Birch asks, "With all these disadvantages in space costs, transportation costs, and taxes, how do we explain the tremendous concentration of economic activity found in today's central cities?"

In answering this question, the author stresses the city's increasing specialization in the service sector as well as the differences in economic strength of cities based on the size and age of their metropolitan areas. Birch concludes that ". . . we can envision a future that is quite different from the past. The central city is no longer able to function as a general-purpose economic system . . . Those organizations which can thrive on the advantages that concentration and a large city government can offer are thriving. Others are leaving or, more importantly, not locating there in the first place."

As economic activity shifts so does population. Cause and effect are difficult to measure but the changes in population characteristics are not. It is these changes which have caused many to despair for the central city as its population since World War II has become increasingly characterized by low income. Thus, the common picture emerged of central cities populated by low-income families, with a small proportion of very high-income people, surrounded by a suburbia of middle- and high-income families. Accompanying this income distribution was a high concentration of black population in the central cities.

Significantly, Birch suggests the trends which produced this pattern may be changing or at least slowing down. Population density in central-city poverty areas declined at a more rapid rate for both white and nonwhite residents in the last half of the 1960's than in the first half. The proportion of high-income families in central cities nearly doubled from 1959 to 1967 — from 7 per cent to 12 per cent; and black population in the suburbs increased at an annual rate of only 0.7 per cent a year from 1960 to 1966, then jumped to a rate of 8.0 per cent from 1966 to 1968. As incomes rise black residents, like whites, apparently move to the suburbs — particularly those with children of school age.

The study offers a mixed picture of developments involving the central city — its economic specialization, the increased movement of low-income people to the suburbs, the search by nonwhites for suburban homes as incomes rise, the growing proportion of higher-income people in the central city. All these factors must be checked against the 1970 census to see whether the preliminary trends are verified by more complete data. The new trends, if confirmed by that census, present opportunities and dangers.

Inner-suburbia densities are approaching those of central cities; central cities may be attracting more high-income people but their economic base is becoming increasingly specialized and therefore highly susceptible to changes in technology; the attraction of suburban areas to the higher-income black population thereby leaving behind a higher proportion of lower-income people in some parts of the central city.

As this shifting of economic activities and population continues, the pressures on all parts of the governmental system will be great, but particular stress will be placed on the local parts. As Birch explains, "To the extent that these many local governments are unable to coordinate their response, the load will be even greater. They may be forced into new forms of local government, whether in 1970 they intend to move in this direction or not."

It is to these new responsibilities which the CED policy statement on *Reshaping Government in Metropolitan Areas* is addressed. Birch's study makes clear just how great the challenge to these governments will be.

Alan K. Campbell, *Project Director*
Dean, The Maxwell Graduate School
    of Citizenship and Public Affairs,
    Syracuse University

Contents

1. Introduction

At the turn of the century, the central city was the city. It was the place where business was concentrated. It was the place where the people who worked in the businesses lived. It was, in short, metropolitan America. The outlying towns were largely self-sufficient communities. Only a wealthy few could afford the train fare and the time required to commute from country to city.

All this, of course, has changed. The businesses and the people have spread out across the cities' boundaries, and long-distance commuting has become a way of life. When we speak of metropolitan America, we now refer to 233 standard metropolitan statistical areas, not to 233 cities.

The expansion has not been uniform. Businessmen who relied heavily on meetings with many different people to get things done kept their offices in the city. Small businesses needing low-cost floor space and a diverse source of suppliers stayed. Large office complexes that required large pools of clerical help could not move easily. Many wealthy families, especially those without children, preferred the concentration of opera houses, restaurants, museums, theaters, and nearby offices, and could afford the high cost of living near them. Many poor families had no alternative but to stay.

On the other hand, manufacturers who could take advantage of cheap land and large, single-level floor space moved out eagerly. Families that wanted more space for their children and

Author's Acknowledgement

No paper of this sort is written alone. I have received invaluable assistance in structuring and editing the paper from Raymond Vernon. Cornelia Lehmann and my wife Louisa were a great help in collecting the data on which so much of the paper is based. Janis Daisey has produced the several drafts leading up to this version. Finally, I am most grateful for the editorial support provided by Carl Rieser of the CED staff and the numerous reviewers whose comments are reflected throughout the paper.

privacy for themselves also left the city. At the same time, many new enterprises and families were formed outside the city rather than within it. Retailers, and eventually wholesalers, sprang up to service them. As a result of this selective relocation, the central city, which was once a concentrated, self-contained economic and residential whole, now finds itself becoming a relatively specialized segment of a rapidly growing area.

The pains and discomforts of conversion have been many. The plight of the poor, trapped, central-city resident has been publicized and has received a great deal of national attention. The congestion of the central cities' streets and the pollution of their water and air have become extreme. The frustrations of central-city mayors, faced with a list of urgent needs and relatively static financial bases, are well known.

A critical question now facing the nation is how, and to what extent, we are going to meet the cities' needs. As a prerequisite to making that decision, we must understand in some detail how the central city is changing and what its probable future course will be. It is difficult to know where to begin. Shifts in employment cannot be considered apart from shifts in population; they are hopelessly intertwined. Jobs seem as logical a starting place as any, however, and this paper will begin with a description of how central-city employment has changed since World War II. As will be seen, the movement of people has been closely related to shifts in employment, and population shifts will be considered in the second main section. Finally, some attempt will be made to assess the strength of the trends affecting central-city development and the probable effect that several changes in policy and technology might have upon these trends.

2. The Changing
Economic Function

As Raymond Vernon pointed out ten years ago,[1] on the surface there is little or no reason why economic activity should be located in the central city. Vernon found that, with a few exceptions, wage rates are practically indistinguishable between central city and suburb. He also found few, if any, advantages for businesses in the city in terms of space costs, transportation costs, and taxes. Manufacturing floor space in the central city is slightly more expensive in small quantities and a great deal more expensive in large quantities. Even taking into account the extra conveniences that must be built into new suburban locations, such as parking, shopping facilities, and cafeterias, space costs are more or less equal between city and suburb.

With rising congestion in the cities, rapid construction of circumferential highways, and the granting of advantageous city rates to suburban shippers, the cost advantage to a manufacturer or wholesaler of a central-city distribution point may no longer be substantial. For a retailer, the bulk of whose customers will not drive more than twenty minutes to get to his store, a central-city location can be a distinct disadvantage. Taxes in the central city are somewhat higher, and the differential can be expected to continue as the cities' needs continue to outstrip their resources.

With all these disadvantages in space costs, transportation costs, and taxes, how do we explain the tremendous concentrations of economic activity found in today's central cities?

The first, and most obvious, explanation is that the central cities are where it all started. In the days when transportation was

---

[1] Raymond Vernon, *The Changing Economic Function of the Central City* (New York: Committee for Economic Development, 1959).

difficult and slow and the advantages of a harbor or a railroad intersection were great, the geographically concentrated city was the best solution for men of affairs and their families. *The* place to close a financial deal was the Cosmopolitan Club or Frank's Delicatessen. Out-of-town guests expected to be entertained at the 21 Club. Investments depreciate slowly and customs change slowly. If the central cities claimed no measurable economic advantages today, we would still not expect the concentrations that developed during the late nineteenth and early twentieth centuries to disperse rapidly.

But we must look beyond historical geography if we are to explain why so many central cities are still growing at a rapid pace. The search for a positive explanation led Vernon to identify three factors: (1) the communication factor, (2) the costs of uncertainty, and (3) the external economies of scale.

As Vernon saw it, face-to-face communication is very important to the small manufacturer who is dealing in a nonstandard product on a tight schedule. The producer of legal briefs or women's clothes or the seller of fresh produce must engage in all the subtleties of showing his product to the customer, reaching an agreement on the spot, and delivering the product — all in a very short period of time. The headquarters of business firms need to be in close personal contact with the bankers, the underwriters, and the stock brokers who provide them with funds, with the lawyers who protect and advise them, with the officers of other firms with whom they do business, and with a host of specialized suppliers. Taken together, the people in these firms constitute a number of closely knit communities that depend upon day-to-day personal communication to get things done. An entire community can be moved physically, as was the produce market in Paris and the garment industry in Amsterdam, but it must remain as a community in order to sustain the human relationships on which it depends.

Minimizing the costs of uncertainty by locating in a congested urban complex is once again primarily the concern of the small producer of nonstandard products. The small machine shop owner or the producer of advertising brochures is constantly seeking new business that may require the use of new materials and processing techniques. The risk of investing in equipment to produce his own materials for any particular order is very great as compared with the short-term savings he might obtain. He would much prefer to be in a position to call on a diversity of competing suppliers, despite the extra cost. Likewise, the man who runs a specialized lathe or printing process needs a great diversity of customers to assure him of steady production. He cannot afford to be dependent upon one or two customers whose individual needs for his special product might vary a great deal. This interacting group of suppliers and producers forms a community in which one relies on the other to minimize risk.

External economies of scale have long been put forth as a rationale for concentration. The city can provide for the smaller firm what the larger, suburban company might have to provide for itself, or do without. The smaller firm contracts, either directly or through taxation, for the partial use of a subway or an airport, a freight distribution service or a sewage disposal plant. Collectively, these smaller firms bargain together for lower shipping rates. They hire a part-time electrician by purchasing his services by the hour. Because the central cities are able to offer this opportunity to share large fixed costs, they serve as breeding grounds for small firms. Vernon was not surprised to find that 69 per cent of small plants were located in central cities, whereas only 45 per cent of their larger, more self-sufficient counterparts were situated in such centers. It is no accident that new firms spring up and die in the central cities at about twice the rate that they do in the suburbs. The ease of getting started is much greater when the burdens of getting started can be shared.

The advantages of close personal communication, lower costs of uncertainty, and external economies of scale are obviously greater for some firms than for others. Wholesalers and service firms, which tend to deal in specialized, nonstandard products, cannot completely ignore the advantages of a central location and thus tend to be more content in the central city. However, retailers, taking advantage of a short shopping radius, and manufacturers, attracted by the efficiencies of single-story plants, have increasingly located in the suburbs.

The City's Increasing Specialization

Attempts to document these observed trends have been frustrated for years because of the inadequate level of detail contained in census and other data. Detailed employment data for most central cities and suburban areas are available only for retail trade, wholesale trade, manufacturing, and selected services, which, in combination, account for only 55 per cent of total metropolitan employment and 58 per cent of central-city employment.

Accepting for the moment these shortcomings, an analysis of the four employment categories for which data are available supports our Darwinian assumption that some forms of activity survive better than others in a central-city environment, and that services survive the best. Looking at Figure 1, we note that, for a sample of seventy-three Standard Metropolitan Statistical Areas (SMSA's), representing 75 per cent of the total metropolitan population,[2] there have been recent absolute declines in retail trade, relatively slow growth in wholesaling and manufacturing, and rather greater growth in service jobs.

As a further check on this pattern, we must look to "other services," a category which includes most nonbusiness organizations, such as hospitals, law offices, schools, and nonprofit membership organizations (ranging from the Knights of Columbus to the Elks to CORE). We must also examine jobs in such fields as finance, insurance, real estate, and government. Together, these additional sectors account for approximately 32 per cent of central-city employment, raising our over-all coverage to about 90 per cent.

---

[2] For a full description of the seventy-three sample SMSA's, see Appendix I, p. 40.

FIGURE 1

Growth of Central City Employment by Major Industry Groups: 1948–1963

Distribution and Mean Annual Percentage Change for Seventy-Three SMSA's

Employment Category	Per Cent of Total Central City Employment in 1963	Mean Annual Percentage Change		
		1948–54	1954–58	1958–63
Retail trade	20.0	0.8	1.8	−0.9
Wholesale trade	5.7	1.6	2.3	1.4
Manufacturing	27.5	3.6ᵃ	1.1	1.6
Selected services	5.0	2.3	4.7	2.4

ᵃData pertain to 1947–1954.

Sources: National Planning Association, Economic and Demographic Projections for Two Hundred and Twenty-Four Metropolitan Areas, Regional Economic Projections Series, Report No. 67-R-1, Vol. I, II, and III; U.S. Department of Commerce, Bureau of the Census, County Business Patterns, 1948, 1956, and 1958; and U.S. Department of Commerce, Bureau of the Census, Census of Manufactures and Census of Business, selected reports for various years, 1954–1963. See Appendix II, p. 41.

Unfortunately, the data for these additional sectors are quite sketchy. There are only eight SMSA's for which central-city statistics are available, and then only because county and city boundaries happen to coincide in these eight instances, thus opening up the detailed data ordinarily available for counties. The figures for the eight cities reveal some support for the concept of growing central-city specialization in service-type jobs. In Figure 2, we note that hospitals, schools, and law offices are growing much more rapidly as a group than is any sector yet examined. The financial sector is also expanding quite rapidly. Government employment is growing more slowly, and there appears to be a trend for insurance and real estate organizations to abandon the city for greener pastures.

If these differential growth rates are as persistent over the next fifteen to twenty years as they have been since 1948 — and

FIGURE 2

Change in Central City Employment by Selected Categories: 1948–1967

Distribution and Mean Annual Percentage
Change for Eight Central Cities[a]

Employment Category	Per cent of Total Central-City Employment in 1963	Mean Annual Percentage Change	
		1948–56	1956–67
Finance	3.1	4.0	4.1
Insurance and real estate	3.9	1.8	−0.2
Government[b]	11.4	n.a.	2.0
Other services[c]	13.4	4.0	15.7

[a]Baltimore, Denver, New Orleans, New York, Philadelphia, St. Louis, San Francisco, and Washington, D.C.
[b]Data pertain to 1957–1962.
[c]Includes medical, legal, educational, and miscellaneous business services, as well as nonprofit membership organizations.
Sources: See Figure 1.

in the absence of dramatic changes in transportation or communication, we have every reason to believe that they will be — then it is reasonable to expect that the central cities will continue to become economic specialists. They will increasingly serve as the home for the hospital, the corporate headquarters, and the state office building.

The degree to which these trends persist will depend, of course, to a certain extent upon the relative growth of the sectors within the economy as a whole. If our greatest expansion as a nation over the next twenty to thirty years were to be in manufacturing or retail trade, rather than services, then the prospects for continued central-city growth would be diminished. However, one comprehensive projection, made by the National Planning Association, suggests otherwise. The NPA estimates summarized in Figure 3 indicate that it is the services (aggregated in this case),

FIGURE 3

Growth of U.S. Employment by Major Categories Since 1950, Projected to 1975

Average Annual Rate of Change

Employment Category	Actual		Projected 1962–75
	1950–57	1957–62	
Retail trade	0.3%	0.8%	1.9%
Wholesale trade	0.9	0.6	1.9
Manufacturing	1.6	−0.3	1.2
Services	2.7	3.5	2.9
Finance insurance and real estate	3.6	2.7	3.2
Federal government	2.2	1.9	0.1
State and local government	3.4	4.5	4.2

Sources: See Figure 1.

the financial community, and the government that can expect the greatest growth through at least 1975.

Thus, it can be assumed from the available evidence that, in aggregate, central cities will experience substantial growth in the white-collar, service-type job categories. As manufacturers, wholesalers, and retailers settle elsewhere, the effect of the growth in services will be to alter the mix of activities going on in central cities, which, in turn, will quite probably have an influence on the kinds of people living there.

The Suburb Versus the City

Before we examine the residential function of cities, there remain two important economic questions. First, how are cities faring relative to suburbs in terms of economic growth rates? A basic consideration here is whether cities are capturing the bulk of the region's service jobs, and hence becoming service centers,

FIGURE 4

Growth of Suburban Employment by Major Industry Groups: 1948–1963

Mean Annual Percentage Change for Seventy-Three SMSA's

Employment Category	1948–1954	1954–1958	1958–1963
Retail trade	1.8%	15.5%	11.3%
Wholesale trade	4.5	17.6	9.4
Manufacturing	10.5[a]	6.3	9.9
Selected services	8.9	18.1	13.8

[a]Data pertain to 1947.
Sources: See Figure 1.

or whether their specialization merely reflects an internal shift. Second, are all cities — large and small, young and old, north, south, and west — behaving in roughly the same fashion, or can we expect differences?

It is clear that the suburbs are growing much faster than the cities, despite the absolute gains of the central cities. As can be seen by a comparison of Figure 4 with Figure 2, suburban growth rates are much higher (sometimes by a factor of ten or more) than those of the central city.

This rapid suburban expansion has had a predictable effect on the central-city share of total metropolitan employment: without exception, the central-city percentage is declining. (See Figure 5.) The difference in the central-city share as between one type of employment and another is less predictable, and perhaps more informative. In particular, the central city's relatively high share of service and financial jobs suggests that the city, by specializing in service work, has been able to attract and hold a great percentage of all high-priced service jobs in the region. It thus appears to be functioning as an elite service center.

FIGURE 5

The Central City's Changing Share of Urban Employment: 1948–1967

Percentage

Employment Category	1948	1954	1956	1958	1963	1967
SAMPLE OF SEVENTY-THREE SMSA's[a]						
Retail trade	78.9%	77.6%		72.4%	64.0%	–
Wholesale trade	87.3	86.4		82.4	78.5	
Manufacturing[b]	65.9	64.4		60.8	57.6	
Selected services	88.6	83.1		79.5	75.0	
SAMPLE OF EIGHT SMSA's[c]						
Other services	81.4		83.6%			72.1%
Finance	90.4		86.8			82.9
Insurance and real estate	92.7		89.2			80.2
Government	n.a.		66.0			59.7

(handwritten margin notes beside the 1967 column: 43.0; 55.8; 73.6 (crossed out) 40.1; 57.7)

[a]Statistics for sample of seventy-three SMSA's described in Appendix I.
[b]Data pertain to 1947.
[c]Statistics for sample of eight SMSA's described in Figure 2.
Sources: See Figure 1.

The Life Cycle of the City

It must be emphasized, however, that not all central cities are undergoing the same kind of transformation at the same rate. If we compare large SMSA's (over 500,000 people) with smaller ones (less than 500,000 people), it is clear that cities in smaller SMSA's are growing much more rapidly than cities in larger SMSA's for each employment category. (See Figure 6.) In particular, manufacturers still appear to find the central cities of smaller metropolitan areas attractive, which would suggest that the problems of locating suitable building sites for efficient, one-story plants are not so acute.

FIGURE 6

Growth of Central City Employment by Size and Age of SMSA: 1948–1963[a]

Percentage Change for Seventy-Three SMSA's by Major Industry Groups

	Old SMSA's	Middle-Aged SMSA's	Young SMSA's	Average
RETAIL TRADE				
Large SMSA's	−11.1%	19.8%	73.5%	4.2%
Smaller SMSA's	−13.0	11.7	26.5	18.6
Average	−11.2	15.7	37.7	9.5
WHOLESALE TRADE				
Large SMSA's	4.1	43.9	111.6	23.6
Smaller SMSA's	17.0	26.5	54.2	42.2
Average	4.9	35.2	67.9	30.5
MANUFACTURING				
Large SMSA's	− 0.8	59.6	284.1	42.0
Smaller SMSA's	−10.9	52.6	89.8	69.9
Average	− 1.4	56.1	136.0	52.3
SELECTED SERVICES				
Large SMSA's	31.5	56.6	162.1	50.6
Smaller SMSA's	21.2	37.8	67.8	54.3
Average	30.9	47.2	90.2	52.0

[a]"Old" SMSA's qualified as SMSA's before 1900; "middle-aged," between 1900 and 1930; and "young," after 1930. "Smaller" SMSA's have a population of less than 500,000; "large" SMSA's contain over 500,000 people.

Sources: See Figure 1.

Size, of course, is only one basis for comparing cities, and it is not a particularly useful one for prediction purposes. Intuitively, we would expect Phoenix and Albany, which are almost identical in size, to have quite different futures. Likewise, we might well anticipate different patterns for such matched pairs as Buffalo and Houston, or San Diego and Cincinnati. For one thing, we would expect the younger city in each case to have lower densities and more room for expansion. In point of fact, the densities of these cities are roughly one-half the densities of the older cities. Furthermore, we would expect the younger cities to be built around road networks, rather than around the railroads and harbors of the earlier cities. The combination of open room for new housing and new plants and the greater efficiency of moving from the one to the other should give these younger cities a distinct advantage in attracting jobs and the people to fill them.

There is nothing to suggest, however, that young cities can avoid the life cycle that older cities have experienced. As today's young cities "fill up," new technology will favor the still newer SMSA's, which will be able to incorporate recent advances from the start. The young cities of 1970 will become the older cities of 2050 and, in the process, more than likely will pass through the typical phases of growth, saturation, and eventually stabilization and decline.

To test this conjecture, SMSA's were further grouped according to the year in which each qualified as an SMSA. The resulting categories were: old (before 1900), middle-aged (1900-1930), and young (after 1930). The results strongly support the life-cycle notion. As can be seen in Figure 6, invariably the older the SMSA, the less rapidly it is growing in economic terms. Of particular interest is the absolute decline of retail trade and manufacturing in the older cities. In sharp contrast is the rapid growth of central-city manufacturing in the younger cities regardless of size. If anything, these young cities are capitalizing on their roads and open spaces to become manufacturing rather than service specialists. And, as might be predicted from a life cycle model, the older a city gets, the less its tendency to rely on manufacturing for growth.

This suggests a sequence whereby younger cities chew up low-density land at a good clip with manufacturing floor space, parking lots, and road networks. The other economic functions develop more slowly. As the city ages and becomes more densely populated, central-city land becomes more expensive, and manufacturing declines in significance, as does retail and wholesale trade. Services, in contrast, appear to thrive on concentration, for all the reasons indicated earlier, and, through a process of self-selection and survival, emerge as the dominant economic force in the older, larger cities. The tendency of central cities to become elite service centers appears, like rheumatism and decaying teeth, to be a strong function of age.

One effect of this life cycle phenomenon will be to redistribute the location of economic activity over time. Most of the younger, growing metropolitan areas are found in the South and the West. Whereas at present these younger areas account for only about 25 per cent of total employment, over time their much greater growth rates will give them an increasing share of the nation's gross national product. Conversely the significance of the large northern metropolitan centers, which served as the nuclei of urban growth during the first half of this century, will decline in a relative sense. Companies will not automatically locate their headquarters in New York or Philadelphia or Chicago. A young man will no longer have to "make it" in *the* big city. There will be a larger number of significant and growing economic concentrations to choose from.

Summarizing, we can envision a future that is quite different from the past. The central city is no longer able to function as a general-purpose economic system. Specialization is taking place within the city and within the SMSA, particularly in the older areas. Those organizations which can thrive on the advantages that concentration and a large city government can offer are thriving. Others are leaving or, more importantly, not locating there in the first place.

The extent to which specialization takes place appears closely related to the age of the area in which the city is located. While central cities in older areas are declining absolutely in most non-service jobs, cities in younger areas are growing quite rapidly across the board. Since the younger areas are located primarily in the South and the West, one result of this life-cycle effect will be to alter substantially the location of economic growth during the next fifty years. The pillars of American urban society during the first half of the century will have to accept a relatively lesser role in the future.

Accompanying this shift in economic activity will be a marked shift in population. The next section focuses upon the resulting changes in the cities' residential function.

3. The Changing
Residential Function

As noted earlier, it is practically impossible to determine cause and effect when examining shifts in economic activity and population. Do firms locate for overriding economic reasons and do people follow to minimize commuting time and cost? Or do people have a natural preference for open space and privacy and thus decide to locate economic activity to suit these preferences? Both factors are at work in any given instance, and the mixture varies for each class of activity. There is some indication that prior to World War II the pattern of commuting from suburb to central cities resulted in a relatively low concentration of jobs in the suburbs, and that after the war jobs were moved closer to places of residence, to the extent that they could be. As a result, a correction took place and jobs grew faster than population in the suburbs. While retail trade and wholesale trade in the suburbs were growing at the rate of 11 per cent and 14 per cent per year, respectively, during the period from 1948 to 1963 and manufacturing and selected services were each growing 19 per cent per year, suburban population was expanding by only 5 per cent per year.

Whatever the explanation, there can be no doubt that people and jobs have both been moving in the same direction — into the suburbs. The rapid redistribution of population that has taken place in the United States during this century is seen in Figure 7, which shows the striking shift from rural to suburban living, with the central city remaining relatively static, as total U.S. population has climbed from 76 million in 1900 to 198 million in 1968. Despite the earlier strong growth of central cities and the relative sleepiness of suburbs from 1900 to 1930, the rapid acceleration of suburban growth following World War II has tended to reduce the central-city share of urban population at an accelerating pace. Whereas in 1920 it was 66 per cent and 59 per cent in 1950, it is now only 45 per cent of total urban population. If present trends persist, and all the evidence regarding job relocation suggests that they will, the central cities can expect that their share will continue to drop, which means that their significance as focal points for their regions will be much diminished by the year 2000.

Because of the significant variations between cities in regard to jobs, it would be surprising if the relative decline of central cities were uniform. And, in fact, it is not. The population of a central city will begin to level off when its economy does. The first signs of this can be seen in Figure 8. Just as the economies of the larger cities have slowed down, so too has their population growth. Cities in the larger SMSA's grew quite rapidly between 1900 and 1920, and then began to level off. The small and medium sized cities slowed somewhat during the Depression, but then rebounded under the stimulus of World War II and the postwar economy.

When age is taken into account in comparing cities of similar size, as in Figure 9, the strong tendency for cities in younger areas to grow faster becomes clear. The younger cities, with their open land and the prospects for rapid economic expansion are attracting proportionately a much greater share of the population. As they fill up and as the expansion of jobs slows down, they become the middle-aged or older cities of a later generation and their attractiveness declines. It is interesting to note that size per se is not necessarily a determining factor in this process. In fact, the most rapidly growing areas are the larger, young cities, such as San Diego, Houston, and Miami, which offer all the advantages of youth as well as the facilities and life style that come with a large city. The precocious city has a promising future.

Since the pattern of population expansion closely resembles the pattern of employment growth, many of the conclusions that we drew for the reallocation of economic activity will probably be true for population as well. If present trends continue, the large northern cities will decline in relative terms, and perhaps abso-

FIGURE 7A

Shift of U. S. Population to Suburbs, 1900-1968

A. Increases in Rural, Urban, and Suburban Populations

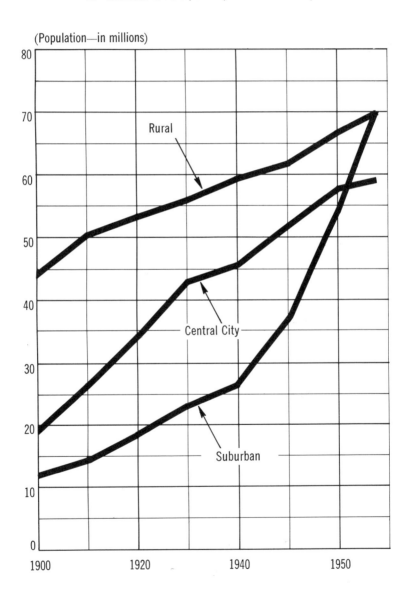

(Population—in millions)

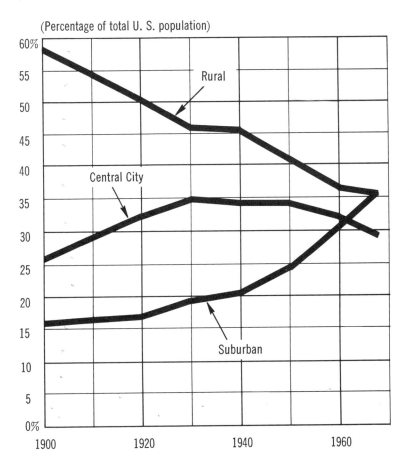

FIGURE 7B

Shift of U. S. Population to Suburbs, 1900-1968

B. Changes in Share of Each Sector

(Percentage of total U. S. population)

Rural

Central City

Suburban

1900   1920   1940   1960

Sources: U.S. Department of Commerce, Bureau of the Census, U.S. Census of Population: 1960, Selected Area Reports, Standard Metropolitan Statistical Areas, Final Report DC (3)-ID; Current Population Reports, Trends in Social and Economic Conditions in Metropolitan Areas, Series P-23, No. 27, February, 1969; and Current Population Reports, Provisional Estimates of the Population of 100 Large Metropolitan Areas: July 1967, Series P-25, No. 411, December, 1968.

FIGURE 8

Growth of Central-City Population
by Size of SMSA: 1900–1960[a]

Mean Annual Percentage
Change for Seventy-Three SMSA's

Size	1900–20	1920–40	1940–60
Large SMSA's	6.48	2.29	1.66
Medium SMSA's	8.47	3.08	3.50
Small SMSA's	9.68	4.54	4.80

[a]"Large" SMSA's, have a population of over 1 million; "medium," between 500,000 and 1 million; and "small," less than 500,000.
Sources: See Figure 7.

FIGURE 9

Growth of Central-City Population
by Size and Age of SMSA: 1920–1960[a]

Mean Annual Percentage
Change for Seventy-Three SMSA's

Size	Old SMSA's	Middle-Aged SMSA's	Young SMSA's	Average
Large SMSA's	1.4%	6.4%	17.8%	4.2%
Smaller SMSA's	0.8	3.5	10.2	7.3
Average	1.4	4.9	12.0	5.3

[a]For definitions of age and size of SMSA's, see Appendix I.
Sources: See Figure 7.

lutely. The growth of their suburbs will also be much slower. Springing up to absorb the bulk of future growth will be the smaller and younger areas, mostly in the South and the West. Since most of the advantages of economic concentration appear to persist, we can expect people to continue to cluster around such concentrations. The prospects for the emergence of entirely new SMSA's, consisting in whole or in part of today's rural areas, would appear to be very great indeed.

Suburban Growth Patterns

In formulating government policy to aid or abet this expansion of metropolitan America, it is not sufficient merely to know where growth will take place. As in the case of jobs, it is equally important to know how and why the expansion takes place. It is clear from the data already presented that the suburbs have been growing very rapidly. By what process has this occurred? Is there anything that is likely to change it? Have all groups been moving into the suburbs at the same rate and, if not, what effects will the differences have on the future of the central city?

To an increasing extent, suburbanites will be born suburbanites. They may move quite often from one suburb to another, but their origin will still be suburban when viewing the nation's population as a whole. There will be some movement into the suburbs, of course, from rural areas, from abroad, or from central cities. All the data on the relocation of jobs suggest that the wealthier of the rural families falling victim to large-scale farming will move directly to a suburb. To a certain extent, this movement will take place automatically as new SMSA's are carved out of rapidly growing rural areas.

Poorer rural laborers on the move, particularly if they are black, are more apt to follow a historical pattern and join the foreign-born immigrants in the central city, where rents are lower and ethnic and racial concentrations greater. The shifting of jobs and the accessibility of deteriorating inner suburbs could well alter the preferences of future poor immigrants, but not completely.

The evidence suggests that, once settled in the central city, regardless of how it gets there, a family will seek a better education for its children and, more often than not, a bigger apartment in a better neighborhood. The scraps of data available reveal that the family will move several times in this search. According to census figures, slightly over half of all central-city families move at least once every five years, and there are many that move more than once. In a rising economy, when jobs are plentiful, the odds are better than even that a family's income will be rising and that it will indeed be moving into a better neighborhood rather than into a worse one. Setbacks are always possible, of course. An individual family might thus have experienced the following pattern of moves:

In 1920, the family moved into Neighborhood A from a farm, from abroad, or possibly from another central city, and lived there for ten years. The neighborhood, already crowded, was running downhill as the housing decayed. Over the ten years, the family's income went up enough to allow the move to Neighborhood B. The gain was only temporary, however, due to the Depression, and our family was forced to move to Neighborhood C. The war years brought the family head a much better job and, by 1952, he was able to move to Neighborhood D, where the family remained until the death of the father or the mother. The children were married by this time, however, and they moved to Neighborhood E, or beyond. In this process, the family has experienced disjointed and probably very frustrating change, but, in economic and social terms, an upward and not a downward movement is suggested by the data.

Meanwhile, the central-city neighborhoods were decaying. Neighborhood A, at one time a nice block of apartment houses, had become a tightly packed slum by the time our family moved there in 1920. By the time the family left, the area had gone downhill still further, and more people were moving out than in. While Neighborhood A was declining, of course, so too were Neighborhoods B, C, D, and E; and, in fact, it is their decay that kept the rents down and facilitated the movement of the family into them.

This facilitating property assumes great importance when we examine where in the region the family started and where it ended up. There is a good chance that the pattern might have looked as follows:

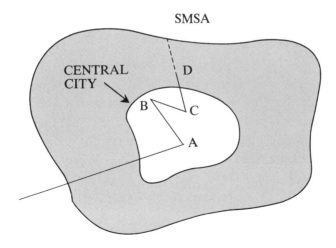

Neighborhood A was in the heart of the central city. By the time our family reached Neighborhood D, it was already a declining suburban community, and the children were thinking of moving farther still. The motivation for this out-movement is already partially in evidence. Jobs are far more plentiful, "reverse" commuting is very difficult and expensive, schools in the suburban area are generally better, and the housing tends to be in better condition.

Not every family follows this path, of course. Some never move, some stay within five miles of their first city home, and some move out and then back. On the average, however, more are moving out than back. This trend shows up in a number of different ways. There has, for example, been an absolute decline in central-city poverty areas — particularly in the large northern cities, such as New York and Detroit — and rapid growth in the adjacent inner suburbs. Recent census data reveal that, even on a nationwide basis, central-city poverty areas have experienced sharp population declines and that, recently, these declines have been almost as great for blacks as for whites, as shown by the following mean annual percentage changes in central city poverty areas:[1]

	1960-1967	1967-1968
White	-2.90	-13.5
Nonwhite	-0.01	- 8.9

A recent study conducted in Massachusetts found that the central-city share of the state's metropolitan poor had declined from 80 per cent in 1950 to 45 per cent in 1967 and that the densities in Boston's inner suburbs, which were absorbing the brunt of the relocation, were equal to the average density of the state's central cities. The sample of seventy-three SMSA's (Figure 10) shows that, for the large SMSA's, total central-city densities have

---

[1] For sources of data, see Figure 7.

FIGURE 10

Change in Population Densities of Central Cities and Suburbs: 1940–1960 for Seventy-Three SMSA's[a]

| | Central Cities | | | Suburbs | | |
	1940	1950	1960	1940	1950	1960
Large SMSA's	10,211	11,146	10,876	329	453	715
Medium SMSA's	6,712	7,589	7,707	142	224	387
Small SMSA's	6,319	7,460	7,675	81	122	188

[a]Density is measured by population per square mile of land area. In order to obtain an accurate picture of shifting density, the effect of central-city annexations were removed from the calculations. Actual central-city densities in 1950 and 1960 are thus somewhat lower than those indicated above.

Sources: See Figure 7.

declined since 1950 and, for the smaller areas, the densities have leveled off. Suburban densities, in contrast, are growing rapidly and, by central-city standards, have enormous potential for future growth.

Decay is thus a double-edged sword. It is disastrous for the family that is rooted to an area and must watch its assets and its environment decline. To a family in search of a better job, a better apartment, and a better school, however, decay, particularly suburban decay, is a great facilitator. It gives the black in Harlem a chance to move to Mount Vernon, if he so chooses, and, as we shall see shortly, many blacks have so chosen.

Age, Income, and Mobility

It is obvious that the ability of families to participate in this immigration process varies a great deal. As might be expected, the result is residential, as well as economic, specialization for the central city. The wealthy family, for example, has more choices than does the poor family. It can pay the high price of comfortable central-city living or it can pay for privacy in a well-to-do suburb. Those with low incomes have less choice; insofar as choice exists, it tends to be between deteriorating neighborhoods in the central city and aging neighborhoods in the inner suburbs. The middle-income groups likewise have fewer choices than do the wealthy. Unable to absorb the costs of a spacious apartment or a townhouse in the city and the costs of private education that go with it, and being unwilling to settle for the less attractive inner suburbs, those in the middle are under considerable pressure to locate long distances from the central city.

This present set of choices does not imply, however, that the central cities must inevitably become the home of the poor. Quite the contrary. As inner suburbs decline to the point where rents are lower but the schools are still better than those in the city, the poor, given the chance, are apt to follow their more affluent predecessors out. It is quite likely that the 1970 census will uncover a suburbanization of the poor in much of the country not unlike that in Massachusetts. At the same time, the economic specialization of the central city offers an increasing incentive for wealthier families to reclaim larger sections of the city for their own use, be it in the form of large new apartment complexes or renovated townhouses. We already see some evidence that both trends are at work. The data in Figure 11 demonstrate that an increasing percentage of central-city residents are in the upper income brackets and that a decreasing percentage have low incomes. The notably sharp increase in the percentage of families with incomes over $15,000, during a period when total central-city population changed very little, suggests that the affluent are fully aware of the advantages of returning to the city.

The age of a family head has also had a significant effect on the ability to move. The older couple and the young teenager are particularly immobile. The young married couple with children, however, is at the point in its career where the opportunity and motivation for moving are both great. The effects of this selective

FIGURE 11

Family Income Distribution in All
U.S. Central Cities: 1959 and 1967

(1967 dollars)

Income Bracket	Percentage 1959	1967
Under $4,000	22%	19%
$4,000–$5,999	20	15
$6,000–$7,999	19	18
$8,000–$9,999	15	15
$10,000–$14,999	16	22
$15,000 and over	7	12
	100%	100%

Sources: See Figure 7.

migration, coupled with the "war baby" phenomenon, have been felt in both the central cities and the suburbs. Figure 12 indicates that, in the cities, the result has been an absolute decline among those twenty-five to forty-four years of age, reflecting their search for better schools, better housing, and better jobs. The war babies, who are in their late teens and early twenties by now, account in part for the growth in the sixteen-to-nineteen and twenty-to-twenty-four age brackets. As this group reaches the "migrating age" during the next five years, however, they will probably follow on the heels of their older brothers and sisters, for all the same reasons, further accelerating the shift from central city to suburb. In addition, we can expect that they will take their children with them, as their brothers and sisters are now doing, and that the absolute decline in the number of young children will continue.

The suburbs are gaining in every age group. They certainly have absorbed their share of war babies. In addition, they are attracting many of the younger couples that the central cities are losing.

FIGURE 12

Growth of Population by Age
for U.S. Metropolitan Areas: 1960–1968

Percentage Change

Age	Central Cities	Suburbs
Under 5	−17.6%	6.7%
5–15	11.3	28.0
16–19	40.8	79.1
20–24	15.1	79.1
25–44	−14.2	14.8
45–64	− 3.9	34.8
65 and over	10.7	46.3

Sources: See Figure 7.

If these trends continue, the city will increasingly become the domain of the elderly. Offsetting this possibility is the return of the affluent, both young and old, and the expansion of service jobs that may hold those already in the city, as well as attracting job-seekers back. It is not at all clear at this point, however, that these factors will halt the over-all decline in the younger age categories. It is more probable that the present problems of recruiting a young, aggressive labor force from a declining supply of potential applicants will persist.

Suburbanization of the Blacks

Of all factors affecting the specialization of population in the central city, none has been greater than race. Faced with all the barriers to jobs and housing resulting from racial prejudice, and starting at the lower rungs of the economic ladder, blacks have participated only to a limited extent in the outward migration. As the following figures demonstrate, relative to the proportion of blacks in the national population, black percentages in the central city are high and rising:[2]

Black population as a proportion of the population of:	1960	1968
Total U.S.	11%	12%
Central Cities	16	20
Suburbs	5	5

If this pattern were to continue, the central cities would become dominated by a black population isolated from the rapid expansion of economic activity in the suburbs and requiring great financial assistance. But if this pattern is being broken and blacks are beginning to follow other ethnic groups before them — first into the less desirable neighborhoods and eventually into the better ones — then the trend of black concentration could well slow down and ultimately reverse itself.

There was little evidence in the 1960 census that blacks were participating in the outward migration, and even a suggestion that those who did leave were worse off than blacks who remained in the city. Nor was there any real indication of change in this pattern through 1965. But recent data, sketchy as they may be, are beginning to suggest that a significant change may now be taking place. The first indication is to be found in the above figures showing the changing percentage of population which is black in cities and suburbs. Earlier we noted the relative stagnation of the central city and the rapid growth in population of the suburbs. The increased central-city concentration of blacks has resulted as much from white out-migration and absolute declines in population as from an increase in black population. By contrast, the steady 5 per cent black concentration in the growing suburbs reflects a rather substantial growth in the number of suburban blacks — from 2.4 million to 3.3 million.

---

[2]/ For sources of data, see Figure 7.

The growth of the suburban black population is seen even more clearly in Figure 13. The jump in the average growth rate of the suburban black population, from 0.7 per cent per year during 1960-1966 to 8.0 per cent per year during 1966-1968, reflects a continuous and sharply increasing black migration into suburban towns. This has happened during the same period that blacks were abandoning central-city poverty areas at a significant rate. It can be conjectured, therefore, that blacks are leaving old neighborhoods and moving into newer ones and that, recently, these moves have pushed across city boundaries in significant numbers. If the concept of a prime "migrating age" operates in the case of blacks, one might expect much of this black movement to be in the twenty-to-thirty age bracket. The experience in Detroit suggests that this is indeed the case. While Detroit's total population under twenty and over thirty is roughly 45 per cent black, only 14 per cent of those twenty to thirty years of age are black.

It is not at all clear, therefore, that black concentrations in central cities will continue to rise. If we assume that retail and manufacturing jobs, on which blacks rely so heavily, will continue to be located outside the city, there is every reason to suppose that the growth of central-city black populations will taper off as the war babies reach their twenties and begin to move out in search of those jobs. Figure 13 suggests that this process may already be at work. The central-city black growth rate has dropped from 3.4 per cent per year to 1.0 per cent per year. If this is coupled with the strong need of wealthy families — black and white — to live near the high-paying service jobs at the city's center, there is the real prospect of a declining black population in the central city and the substantial reuse of present ghetto areas.

The relocation of blacks is, of course, only part of the story. If the quality of black life does not improve in the process, then the only effect would be to transfer some of the central-city problems to the suburbs.

Although the evidence is again sketchy, at least it consistently points in the same direction — by most social and economic measures, suburban blacks are increasingly better off than their

FIGURE 13

Change in White and Black Populations of Urban Areas: 1960–1966 and 1966–1968

Mean Annual Percentage Change

	1960–66	1966–68
CENTRAL CITIES		
White	−0.3	−1.0
Black	3.4	1.0
SUBURBS		
White	3.0	2.0
Black	0.7	8.0

Sources: See Figure 7.

FIGURE 14

Educational Attainment of Younger Urban Dwellers: 1960 and 1968

Median Years of School Completed by Whites and Blacks
Twenty-Five to Twenty-Nine Years Old

	Central Cities		Suburbs	
	1960	1968	1960	1968
MALES				
White	12.6	12.7	12.5	12.7
Black	11.3	12.3	11.1	12.4
FEMALES				
White	12.4	12.5	12.4	12.6
Black	11.5	12.2	9.9	12.3

Sources: See Figure 7.

FIGURE 15

Median Income of Urban Males
by Educational Attainment; 1959 and 1967

White and Black Males
Twenty-Five to Fifty-Four Years Old

Years of School Completed	Median Income in 1967 (thousands of dollars)		Black Median Income as a per cent of white	
	White	Black	1959	1967
CENTRAL CITY				
Elementary: 8 yrs. or less	5.7	4.2	67%	75%
High School: 1–3 years	6.7	5.1	70	75
4 years	7.5	5.6	69	75
College: 1 year or more	9.2	7.0	65	76
4 years	10.3	7.6	n.a.	74
SUBURBAN RINGS				
Elementary: 8 yrs. or less	6.5	4.0	50%	62%
High School: 1–3 years	7.5	4.6	64	62
4 years	8.2	6.0	64	73
College: 1 year or more	10.5	7.3	59	70
4 years	11.5	n.a.	n.a.	n.a.

Sources: See Figure 7.

central-city counterparts. In terms of educational level attained, blacks in general have come a long way toward narrowing the gap with whites. (See Figure 14.) Furthermore, while in 1960 central-city blacks completed more years of school than suburban blacks, the opposite is now true.

Applying quantitative rather than qualitative standards to education may well overstate actual black gains, which would explain, in part, the lower incomes of blacks in each educational category. (See Figure 15.) However, the recent, rapid gains of blacks relative to whites in practically every category suggest that discrimination is as much a factor as education in influencing in-

FIGURE 16

Children Under Eighteen
Living with Both Parents in Urban Areas

Percentage According to Family Income Bracket

Family Income	Total	White	Black
Under $4,000	36%	51%	24%
$4,000–$5,999	74	78	67
$6,000–$7,999	89	91	80
$8,000–$9,999	93	94	89
$10,000–$14,999	95	96	93
$15,000 and over	96	97	95

Sources: See Figure 7.

come level and that successful efforts to encourage equal-opportunity employment will go a long way toward eliminating income differences.

The effect of gains in education and opportunity on black income distributions has been quite marked. A pool of relatively well-to-do blacks has been developing rapidly in both the central city and the suburbs. Accompanying this rise in income has been an increase in family stability. As can be seen in Figure 16, black families in higher income brackets are practically indistinguishable from their white counterparts in terms of family structure.

From this evidence we might conjecture that the children of the black migrants of the 1940's and the 1950's are taking advantage of better education and less job discrimination to increase their incomes and are likewise establishing far more stable family units than the ones in which they were brought up. As previously noted, many of these young couples, mostly in their early twenties, are now leaving the city for the suburbs and are taking their young children with them.

Spreading Enclaves

Quite apart from the improvement in life style, there remains the question of whether or not blacks are moving from one segregated neighborhood to another. A recent survey conducted by the Survey Research Center of the University of Michigan's Institute of Social Research suggests that there is a strong tendency for blacks to move to existing black neighborhoods, creating enclaves similar to the Italian, German, Polish, and Jewish enclaves created by earlier migrations.

A complete trial run of the 1970 census conducted in New Haven, Connecticut, in 1967 suggests a similar pattern. While the black migration into the suburbs in New Haven is somewhat greater than that for the nation as a whole, the pattern is the same.[3] Figure 17 is a computer-drawn contour map of the region.

While all this recent evidence on black migration is spotty and subject to confirmation by the 1970 census, it all points in the same direction. Blacks finally appear to be moving throughout the metropolitan region in something like the way that other immigrants did before them. As educational opportunities have improved, as jobs have opened up, and as incomes have risen, blacks seem to be forming stable family units, and those units are moving into better neighborhoods as fast as they can.

If this trend is indeed taking place, as all evidence suggests it is, the central city is unlikely to become black dominated. As many poorer blacks follow jobs out into the suburbs and as the central city becomes specialized economically, requiring a highly educated elite — black and white — we can anticipate increased pressure for the rebuilding of present ghetto neighborhoods to serve the needs of this elite. Likewise, we can anticipate a gradual decline of the younger black generation in the central city, its emergence in the inner suburbs, and, as black income increases

---

[3] While the nation was averaging 0.7 per cent per year from 1960-1966 and 8.0 per cent per year during 1966-1968, New Haven was averaging 19.9 per cent per year growth in suburban black population during the entire interval.

FIGURE 17

Concentrations of the Black Population in the New Haven Region, 1967

Figure 17 is a computer drawn contour map of the New Haven region. The higher the elevation, the greater the concentration of blacks. What can be seen from the map is a pattern of enclaves, with a heavy black concentration in the center and signs of assimilation at the fringes. The enclaves are scattered throughout the region and do not merely surround the central city.

still further, its entry in today's outer, wealthier suburbs. Left behind will be the older black couple. These changes will take place slowly, particularly in large cities, and will be very painful for many people. All the evidence suggests, however, that the process is now at work and that it will continue for some time to come.

The effect of these shifts on the inner suburbs and, eventually, on the outer suburbs may be quite dramatic. Already, inner-suburb densities are approaching those of central cities, and increasingly this density growth is attributable to the poor and the blacks. These inner suburbs can thus expect to experience many of the same problems experienced by the central cities during the first half of this century, and, in fact, they may resemble today's central cities in many ways.

The manner in which the suburbs respond to their new populations will have a great effect upon the speed with which the relocation of the poor and the blacks takes place. In Massachusetts, where recently the legislature has been willing to go as far as to require each town to commit 1.5 per cent of its useable land to low- and moderate-income housing, the shift has been and will continue to be quite rapid. In other areas, state and local governments will go to great extremes to resist the entry of new groups. The tide appears to be against them, however. As these new groups enter and grow in size, a tremendous load will be placed upon local governments. To the extent that these many local governments are unable to coordinate their response, the load will be even greater. They may be forced into new forms of government, whether they intended to move in this direction in 1970 or not.

4. Conclusion

Pulling all these interwoven threads together, the future course of the central cities is not totally uncertain. The cities are becoming and will continue to become specialized. Absolute declines in many types of jobs will be offset by substantial gains in communication-sensitive activities, such as banking, corporate headquarters, educational and health facilities, nonprofit membership organizations, and the specialized manufacturing and service firms that service these growth sectors.

Economic specialization is taking place faster in the older, larger, established urban centers than in the younger, smaller ones. The younger central cities are experiencing rapid growth in all sectors, although, as they mature, we can expect specialization to increase.

With economic specialization has come selected groups of people — a shifting mixture of the new and the old. Many of the present residents have every reason to avoid the central city, and the indications are that they have been doing so whenever possible. Barriers against the movement of the poor and the black have been declining as the inner suburbs decline and the incomes of these groups rise. The old are perhaps the least mobile.

Moving in to share the city with this declining, elderly population is a new group. These are the white-collar workers, whose skills are increasingly in demand in the central city and whose commuting time from the suburbs is rising. They are attracted to large, new apartment houses built on vacated land or to renovated, older houses that were built to last in the fashionable neighborhoods of 1900.

The cumulative effect of these economic and residential changes will be to transfer many of the present problems of the central city to the suburbs, particularly the inner suburbs. In the

37

older regions, this is already happening. In Massachusetts, there are now more poor in the state's suburbs than in its central cities, and the suburban share is growing fast.

Considering the millions of decisions and the billions of dollars that are responsible for the trends just described, it is unlikely that government programs on the scale of the 1960's would significantly alter the nature of the changes taking place. It is well to know, however, how existing and future programs might affect these changes, in order both to make more effective use of what we have and to allocate more whenever it might become available.

First, it should be clear that any program that raises the incomes of the poor will accelerate the out-migration of the present city population and thereby facilitate the growth of the new. Programs of this sort might range from direct subsidies provided through welfare, rent supplements, or tax reform to indirect subsidies in the form of increased mortgage availability on multiunit structures, lower interest rates, or suburban highway construction.

Second, any program that makes it easier to recapture large parcels of central-city land will have the same effect. This assumes, of course, that the program makes provisions for minimizing personal hardship and the political protest that usually results when people are asked to move.

Finally, any change in the pattern of government spending that provides further stimulus to those industrial sectors most likely to relocate outside the central city would accelerate the movement of jobs and people.

Of equal, if not greater, significance than government programs are advances in technology. If all the subtleties of face-to-face communication could be captured in a three-dimensional picture phone and if cheap overnight delivery could be guaranteed from any door in the United States to any other door, many of the current advantages of the central city, which form the basis for its projected growth, would be lost. Absolute declines would then become more common.

Likewise, if the time and money required to transport a family head from any home to any place of work could be significantly reduced, the present constraints on metropolitan expansion would be reduced and a far more even distribution of population would result. Once again, the relative position of the central city would decline far more rapidly than predicted.

In the absence of such changes in technology, however, and assuming only modest government efforts to reallocate income and land use, we can expect most central cities to continue to become specialized economically and residentially and to continue to grow. While the younger, smaller cities will grow more easily and the older, larger cities will experience greater pain in transforming themselves from the old to the new, the net result will still be growth. In the process, the central-city crises of the 1960's may well arise as the suburban crises of the 1970's.

Appendix

I

The sample of seventy-three SMSA's was chosen to include the fifty largest SMSA's as of 1960 and, in addition, the twenty largest SMSA's in each of the age categories used for analysis purposes; i.e., those SMSA's that qualified as SMSA's prior to 1900, those qualifying between 1900 and 1930, and those that have become SMSA's since 1930. The result is a sample of seventy-three SMSA's that contained 75 per cent of the total metropolitan population in 1960. In addition to being grouped by age, the SMSA's have been grouped by size: large (over 1 million); medium (between 500,000 and 1 million); small (less than 500,000). They have also been grouped by region: north, south, and west.

With the exception of Figure 2, no adjustments have been made for annexations by central cities. One purpose of the analysis is to determine whether or not the political entity called the central city has been able to attract jobs and people. To the extent that annexations alter the boundaries of the central city, they are relevant and should not be ignored. Another purpose of the analysis, of course, is to determine the future prospects for economic concentration per se. For this purpose, it would theoretically be more accurate to keep the boundaries static around concentrated areas and to analyze the contents within those boundaries over a period of time. Unfortunately, there are no boundaries that ring economic concentrations consistently. In particular, central-city boundaries vary widely in their contents. The city of San Diego, for example, contains many thousands of acres of desert. In the absence of an effective boundary, the varying central-city boundary is used because it meets the first objective and, at the same time, provides a reasonably accurate picture of how the economic concentrations in the center of our SMSA's are performing. If there is any bias, it is to overstate somewhat the growth of the southern and western cities, where annexation has been more prevalent.

II

Following is the list of reports providing data for Figures 1-6:
U. S. Bureau of the Census. *Census of Business:* 1954. Vol. II, *Retail Trade-area Statistics;* Vol. IV, *Wholesale Trade-Area Statistics;* Vol. VI, *Selected Services-Area Statistics.*

——. *Census of Business: 1958.* Vol. II, *Retail Trade-Area Statistics;* Vol. IV, *Wholesale Trade-Area Statistics;* Vol. VI, *Selected Services-Area Statistics.*

——. *Census of Business: 1963.* Vol. II, *Retail Trade-Area Statistics;* Vol. V, *Wholesale Trade-Area Statistics;* Vol. VII, *Selected Services-Area Statistics.*

——. *Census of Manufactures: 1947.* Vol. III, *Area Statistics.*

——. *Census of Manufactures: 1954.* Vol. III, *Area Statistics.*

——. *Census of Manufactures: 1958.* Vol. III, *Area Statistics.*

——. *Census of Manufactures: 1963.* Vol. III, *Area Statistics.*

——. *Census of Business: 1947.* Vol. V, *Wholesale Trade-Area Statistics.*

——. *Census of Business: 1948.* Vol. III, *Retail Trade-Area Statistics;* Vol. VII, *Selected Services-Area Statistics.*

About CED ...

The Committee for Economic Development (CED) is an independent research and educational organization of 200 leading businessmen and educators. With the help of advisory boards of distinguished economists and social scientists, CED trustees conduct research and formulate policy recommendations in four major areas of public policy: (1) the national economy, (2) the international economy, (3) education and urban development, and (4) the management of federal, state, and local government.

CED is nonprofit, nonpartisan, and nonpolitical. It is supported largely by contributions from business, foundations, and individuals. CED's objective is to promote stable growth with rising living standards and increasing opportunities for all Americans.

The Committee for Economic Development draws its 200 trustees largely from the ranks of board chairmen and presidents of business corporations and financial institutions, and from the ranks of university presidents. These trustees are chosen for their individual capacities, for their understanding of public problems, and for their willingness to view these problems from the standpoint of the general welfare and not from that of any special interest group.

All CED policy recommendations must be approved by a fifty-man group of trustees, the Research and Policy Committee, which alone can speak for the organization. These recommendations are set forth in Statements on National Policy and are the result of months of research, discussion, and policy formulation.

In connection with the publication of a statement, CED often publishes documents originally prepared by scholars as background papers but deemed worthy of wider circulation, as in the case of the present Supplementary Paper. Though publication of such papers must be authorized by an editorial board of trustees and academic advisors as a contribution to knowledge, the opinions and conclusions expressed are solely those of the individual authors and do not reflect the policies or views of the trustees.